The Nature in Close-up Series

Richards, Alan
    Woodland Birds.——(Nature in close-up)
    1. Forest birds——Great Britain——
Juvenile literature
I. Title   II. Series
598.2941   QL690.G7

ISBN 0–7136–2589–9

Acknowledgements

Photographs by Aquila Photographics
J Anthony (p 20); S & B A Craig (p 14); E A Janes (pp2, 6); M & V Lane
(Front cover, 7, 18); D I McEwan (p 2 inset); A T Moffett (p 4); R Siegal
(p 21); D S Whitaker (p 23); M C Wilkes (Back cover, pp 5,8,9,10,11,12,
13,15,16,17,19,22).

Artwork by Bob Bampton

Published by A & C Black (Publishers) Limited
35 Bedford Row, London WC1R 4JH

First published 1985
© 1985 A & C Black (Publishers) Ltd

ISBN 0-7136-2589-9

Filmset by August Filmsetting, Haydock, St Helens.
Printed in Hong Kong by Dai Nippon Printing Co. Ltd

Nature in Close-up

WOODLAND BIRDS

Alan Richards

A & C Black · London

Contents

Different kinds of woodland

A wood is a very good place in which to observe bird life. A lot of common woodland birds – blue tits, blackbirds, thrushes – adapted to life in towns when man destroyed the trees they lived in. Some more unusual birds such as redstarts or tree-creepers you will find only in a woodland setting. You can read about them and some of the more common birds in the first part of this book.

All the birds mentioned so far live in *deciduous* woods, that is, forests of trees such as oak, beech and ash which lose their leaves in autumn. These woods have lots of insect life and therefore attract many different kinds of bird. The other type of woodland is *coniferous* woodland, where trees such as Scots pines and Norwegian spruces (called *conifers*) shed and replace their needle-like leaves all the year round.

Most coniferous woods in Britain have been planted by man. They do not harbour many birds but you can read about the most interesting ones in the second part of the book.

(top right) A coniferous plantation in Scotland ▶

Bluebells in a deciduous wood in the south of England ▶

Green woodpecker

Length: 32 cm approx.

The green woodpecker is the easiest of all the woodpecker family to spot, because it is the largest and most brightly coloured. You can tell the male from the female by his red 'moustache'. The female's face is all black.

Woodpeckers cling to the bark of trees, so they need strong feet and stiff tail feathers to balance themselves. They bore holes in tree trunks for their nests, which are often made of just a few wood shavings. Young woodpeckers are speckled, not at all like their parents.

Although the green woodpecker is mainly a tree bird, you might sometimes see it feeding on the ground. It pokes its long sticky tongue into ants' nests to get at the insects and their eggs.

4

Great spotted woodpecker

Length: 23 cm approx.

This bird is the noisiest woodpecker. Listen for the rapid drumming sound as it hammers away at the tree trunk with its sharp beak. This sound is most often heard in the spring from February to May, but you can hear it at other times too.

The woodpecker in this photograph is a female. The male has a red patch on the back of his neck.

Woodpeckers feed on insects and their eggs, which they find in the bark of trees. They also like nuts, which they wedge in the tree bark so that they can pick out the kernels. If a great spotted woodpecker visits your garden, leave out some suet or nuts for it.

5

Nuthatch

Length: 14 cm approx.

The nuthatch is an acrobat. It can move in all directions – even head first and upside down – holding on to the bark with its strong feet. Unlike the woodpecker, it doesn't need its tail to help it to balance. The nuthatch has a pointed beak for picking out the kernels from nuts which it wedges in cracks in the tree bark.

The nuthatch does not bore its own nest-hole, so it chooses a natural hole or one that has been left by a woodpecker. If the hole is too big, the nuthatch plasters mud around the edge so it is just big enough for the tiny bird to squeeze through. The nest is now safe from the attacks of larger birds and animals. Listen for the nuthatch's cheerful whistle. It sounds like 'chuit – chuit – chuit'.

Tree-creeper

Length: 13 cm approx.

The tree-creeper looks rather like a small, brown mouse. It moves jerkily up the tree trunk or sideways, looking for insects and grubs which it picks out of the bark with its curved beak. Once it has explored one tree it moves quickly on to another, and starts all over again.

Tree-creepers usually build their nests behind loose pieces of bark, or amongst branches or ivy. The nest is made of twigs, moss, roots and grass, and lined with wool and hair. They lay about 6 white eggs with red-brown markings.

In winter, tree-creepers sometimes spend the night away from home. They look for a convenient hole in the tree bark, or if the bark is soft enough they dig one out for themselves.

Blue tit

Length: 11 cm approx.

You will all have seen blue tits on your garden bird-table. They also live in woods, especially ones with a lot of oak trees. In the nesting season they fly from branch to branch searching underneath leaves for insects, grubs and caterpillars – food for the baby blue tits. In woods blue tits build their nests in holes in trees, though in gardens they will choose any convenient hole – a drainpipe or letter box, for example.

Blue tits like to keep together in family parties. In the late summer they often fly in groups calling to each other as they search for food.

The blue tit has a relation – the great tit. This bird is about 3 cm bigger than the blue tit, and has a black cap instead of a blue one.

▲ Marsh tit   ▲ Willow tit

Marsh tit and Willow tit

Length: 12 cm approx.

Only real experts can tell these two apart. They
both have black heads, with paler bodies. But if
you look more closely you will see that the marsh tit
has a glossy cap while the willow tit's is a duller
black. When its wings are folded, the willow tit
looks paler in colour. Perhaps the easiest way to tell
them apart is to listen to their calls. The willow tit
sings 'zi – zurr zurr, zi – zurr, zi – zurr' and can be
heard at any time of the year. The marsh tit sounds
more like 'pitchuu – pitchuu' or 'tchair – tchair'.

Both nest in damp marshy places. The willow tit
often digs a nest-hole in soft, rotten tree stumps
(not necessarily willows). The marsh tit prefers to
use a natural hole.

9

Nightingale

Length: 16.5 cm approx.

The nightingale is well known for its singing voice. The best time to hear it is at night when everything is quiet. Listen for the repeated notes ending in a loud burst of song. You can sometimes hear it in the daytime during the summer if you listen carefully.

The nightingale is a *migrant*. It arrives in April and builds its nest in a safe place in a tangle of brambles. It lives on a diet of worms, insects and spiders as well as fruit and berries.

Nightingales are shy birds. They are hardly ever seen and when they do come out their dull feathers make them difficult to spot amongst the trees.

Song thrush

Length: 23 cm approx.

The song thrushes that live in towns feed mostly on worms which they pull up from lawns. In woods they look for insects, snails and spiders, and in winter will eat berries if insects are in short supply. Like the blackbird, the thrush uses mud for its nest, but does not line it. The thrush's eggs are blue with a few speckles and blotches of black on them. Often two or three broods of chicks are raised in the same nest.

Thrushes are especially known for their song, which can be heard from the early winter months until July.

Spotted flycatcher
Length: 14 cm approx.

Spotted flycatchers migrate to warmer countries during the winter and arrive in Britain at the end of April. The adult bird is not spotted; it is mouse brown. The young birds are speckled before they shed their baby feathers and become like their parents. Look for the flycatcher flying jerkily along a leafy woodland path in search of the butterflies and moths on which it feeds.

Flycatchers build their nests on ledges, in holes in tree trunks, or hidden amongst ivy. The nest is made of moss, wool, hair and cobwebs, lined with roots, hair and a few feathers. The 4 to 5 eggs are green with chestnut-coloured spots.

Pied flycatcher

Length: 13 cm approx.

As well as catching insects in flight, the pied flycatcher quite often feeds on the ground, picking up caterpillars from leaves. The male and female look quite different. The male is handsome, with black and white feathers, while the female is dull brown. These flycatchers are fairly common in oak woods and in hilly country where there are rivers and streams. If you live in Wales, the Lake District or parts of South-West England you should almost certainly see one.

As well as nesting in holes in trees, they will also build their homes in garden nesting boxes. Their nests are rather loosely built of bark, moss and roots, lined with hair, wool or feathers, and their eggs are pale blue.

Blackcap

Length: 14 cm approx.

The blackcap in this photograph is a male bird. The female's head is reddish-brown. Blackcaps are difficult to spot because they usually hide in bushes, or amongst honeysuckle or brambles. Although most of them migrate during the winter months, some stay behind and in bad weather you might occasionally find one on your garden bird-table. Blackcaps lay 4 to 5 light brown eggs, blotched with darker brown. They feed mainly on insects, fruit and berries. The blackcap is well known for its rich warbling song.

Redstart

Length: 14 cm approx.

The male redstart attracts its mate by moving its orangey-red tail up and down. Look out for a brightly coloured bird flitting from branch to branch, feeding on insects, spiders, worms and berries. Redstarts like to build their nests in holes in trees, so they usually choose very old ones that have plenty of cracks and crannies. They lay 5 to 7 pale blue eggs with small red spots on them.

Jay
Length: 34 cm approx.

Often, all you will see of a jay is the flash of its blue wings as it flies off with a loud squawk. When it is still, it has the habit of fanning its black tail and swinging it from side to side. It can also raise or lower the black and white crest on its head. Jays like to eat acorns. They collect them in the autumn and bury them to eat in the winter when food is scarce. They also hunt for insects, worms, fruit and berries, and sometimes other birds' eggs. A jay's nest can often be seen in the fork of a tree, about 5 to 6 metres from the ground. It is made of twigs and looks rather untidy. In it the female jay lays 5 to 6 greenish-brown eggs with mottled patches.

Sparrowhawk

Length: 28–38 cm approx.

This fierce-looking bird is a male sparrowhawk. The female is larger and has brownish feathers on her back instead of grey. The sparrowhawk is a bird of prey: it catches small birds and animals in its sharp claws, or talons. If you spot a heap of feathers or fur on a tree stump or mound it might be a sparrowhawk's 'plucking post' – the place where the bird rips its prey to pieces before devouring it.

The sparrowhawk's nest is an untidy platform of twigs built well above ground, about 20 metres or more high in the tree tops. The 5 to 6 eggs are bluish-white or pale green, blotched or streaked with chocolate brown.

17

Wood pigeon

Length: 41 cm approx.

Do not mistake the wood pigeon for its dull grey relative found in towns and suburbs. Although it looks greyish from a distance, closer up it has a darkish-pink breast, with a white patch on its neck. A shy bird, it usually flies off with a clatter of wings when it is disturbed, though sometimes it can become quite tame if it is not startled suddenly.

Farmers do not like wood pigeons and often shoot them because of the damage they do to crops. Wood pigeons build flimsy nests of twigs – usually in bushes or trees about a metre from the ground. The female wood pigeon feeds her young on a kind of 'milk' from her crop (or throat).

Tawny owl

Length: 38 cm approx.

Owls roost during the day in a hole in a tree trunk or thick bush, and come out at night to hunt small animals such as mice, shrews and occasionally small birds and frogs. On a quiet night their hooting can be easily heard from mid-January to June. Owls sometimes take over the old nests of other birds and animals such as crows or squirrels. They lay 2 to 4 glossy white eggs, usually in early March.

Coniferous woodland

Trees such as pines, larches, firs and spruce are called *conifers*. The only conifers that naturally grow in Britain are Scots pines, but forests of Norwegian spruce have been planted on hillsides in Scotland and Wales. Birds do not find this type of coniferous forest very good to live in because it does not offer a wide enough variety of different trees for nesting and feeding. They prefer natural pine forests, and in those you will find a greater number of different birds.

Coal tit

Length: 11cm approx.

This is the smallest member of the tit family, and is common in coniferous plantations. Coal tits often feed together in large flocks, picking insects from the branches of trees with their slender beaks. They are quite easy to spot because of the white patches on the backs of their necks.

The coal tit builds its nest in a hole in a tree trunk or sometimes on the ground. It will also use a nesting box if one is provided.

Goldcrest
Length: 89 mm approx.

The goldcrest is the smallest bird in Europe. The male has a bright orange crest bordered with black, though it is rarely seen. Usually you will only hear its high-pitched cry as it feeds on the tops of trees, looking for insects and spiders. Its tiny nest of moss and spiders' webs hangs like a hammock from the ends of branches. In it the female lays 7 to 8 pale brown eggs with darker brown, fine markings. The goldcrest has a relation – the firecrest – which has a black and white stripe above its eye, as well as an orange crest. This bird is very rare in Britain.

Crossbill
Length: 16.5 cm approx.

The crossbill gets its name from its curious crossed beak, which it uses to extract seeds from fir cones – its favourite food. It holds the cone with one foot and then forces the scales apart to get at the fruit. When a large flock of crossbills is feeding you can hear the sound of cone scales being cracked, and a shower of seed wings and cones drops on to the ground below. Crossbills build their nests early in the year, sometimes laying their eggs in January or February. The nests are built of pine twigs, lined with fur, hair and feathers.

23

Nuthatch

Marsh tit

Tree-creeper

Blue tit

Jay

Nightingale

Green woodpecker

Pied flycatcher

Spotted flycatcher

Great spotted woodpecker

Song thrush

Willow tit

Sparrowhawk

Tawny owl

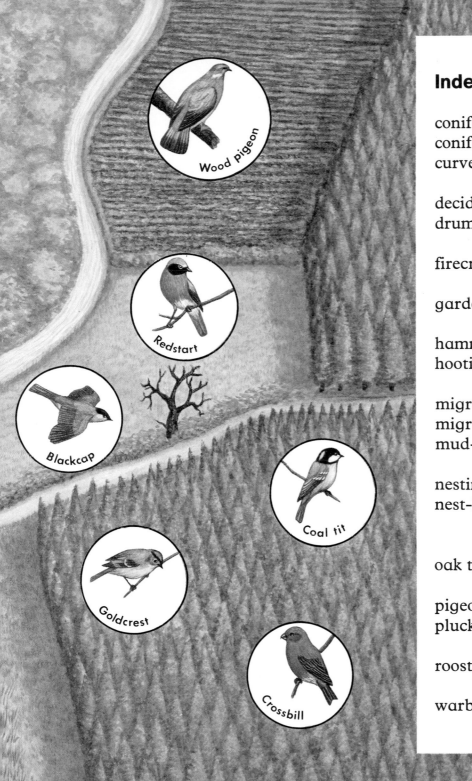

Index